White Soul Mirror Note book

Published by Faulks Books

The Seshen School of Hermetic Meditation is an online school for those following the works of Franz Bardon.

Please visit www.martinfaulks.com for more details.

SCORE CHART FOR THE ELEMENTS

Introduction

The White Soul Mirror notebook is designed to assist you, the practitioner, in the further development and refinement of your character. Used in conjunction with the Black Soul Mirror, the purpose of the White Soul Mirror is to focus on the positive virtues and qualities pertaining to each element. This allows you to investigate and explore aspects of this nature in order to achieve a balance of the four elements. These include virtues that you have already obtained or gained awareness of. The contents of the Soul Mirror points to qualities that may have not entered into awareness as yet and may include potential virtues that you will further cultivate in the future.

The elements are listed in the following order: Earth, Water, Air and Fire respectively. Each element is further divided into three sections, to begin with the smallest quality, then medium, and finally largest.

Within the White Soul Mirror the focus of each elemental section is to record the positive qualities and virtues specific to the element that have already been obtained. Specifically, these include effective strategies, strengths and virtues that you are already proficient in, such as good habits, skills, qualities that create or maintain harmony.

First Section - Small Qualities

These pertain to virtues that are of day to day occurrences that bring harmony to a situation with and have a small impact on our lives. An example of a small Earth element quality would be to have the ability of waking up on time.

Second Section – Medium Qualities

These are virtues of a larger nature which not only impact upon our lives, but also others. A medium Air quality would be the virtue of correct language, speaking in an appropriate manner according to the given situation.

Third Section – Large Qualities

These could be virtues that you have achieved proficiency in, that have a large impact on the lives of others and oneself, for example the leadership to manage and be responsible for a large team of people could be seen as a large virtue of the Fire element.

Attributing Scores to the Elements

Once the appropriate qualities have been added to the Soul Mirror, it is necessary to attribute a collective score to each element, see fig. 1 for example. Thus allowing a greater assessment of the traits and an insight into which element is most prominent, aiding you in the development of equipoise.

Method of Scoring

A suggested method of scoring, is to add a number based on the quality and quantity attributed to that particular virtue. For example,

1= Small Qualities

2= Medium Qualities

3= Large Qualities

Once the qualities and virtues have been added next to the appropriate element and a score attributed to each one of them. Total up the scores for each element and record them on the score sheet provided at the front of the book. This will provide a useful insight into which element is predominant within your personality and assist in a greater understanding of oneself.

Fig. 1 Example Score Chart

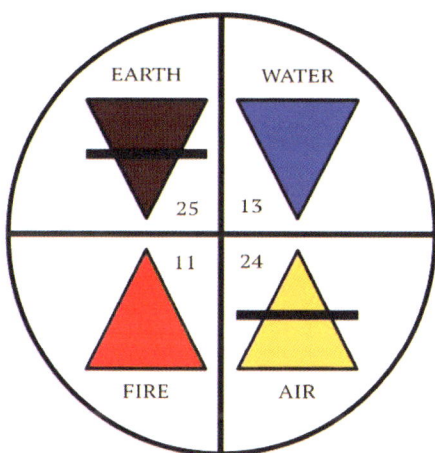

EARTH ELEMENT

SMALL POSITIVE QUALITIES

EARTH ELEMENT

SMALL POSITIVE QUALITIES

EARTH ELEMENT

SMALL POSITIVE QUALITIES

EARTH ELEMENT

SMALL POSITIVE QUALITIES

EARTH ELEMENT

SMALL POSITIVE QUALITIES

EARTH ELEMENT

SMALL POSITIVE QUALITIES

EARTH ELEMENT

SMALL POSITIVE QUALITIES

EARTH ELEMENT

SMALL POSITIVE QUALITIES

EARTH ELEMENT

SMALL POSITIVE QUALITIES

EARTH ELEMENT

SMALL POSITIVE QUALITIES

EARTH ELEMENT

MEDIUM POSITIVE QUALITIES

EARTH ELEMENT

MEDIUM POSITIVE QUALITIES

EARTH ELEMENT

MEDIUM POSITIVE QUALITIES

EARTH ELEMENT

MEDIUM POSITIVE QUALITIES

EARTH ELEMENT

MEDIUM POSITIVE QUALITIES

EARTH ELEMENT

MEDIUM POSITIVE QUALITIES

EARTH ELEMENT

MEDIUM POSITIVE QUALITIES

EARTH ELEMENT

MEDIUM POSITIVE QUALITIES

EARTH ELEMENT

MEDIUM POSITIVE QUALITIES

EARTH ELEMENT

MEDIUM POSITIVE QUALITIES

EARTH ELEMENT

LARGE POSITIVE QUALITIES

EARTH ELEMENT

LARGE POSITIVE QUALITIES

EARTH ELEMENT

LARGE POSITIVE QUALITIES

EARTH ELEMENT

LARGE POSITIVE QUALITIES

EARTH ELEMENT

LARGE POSITIVE QUALITIES

EARTH ELEMENT

LARGE POSITIVE QUALITIES

EARTH ELEMENT

LARGE POSITIVE QUALITIES

EARTH ELEMENT

LARGE POSITIVE QUALITIES

EARTH ELEMENT

LARGE POSITIVE QUALITIES

EARTH ELEMENT

LARGE POSITIVE QUALITIES

WATER ELEMENT

SMALL POSITIVE QUALITIES

WATER ELEMENT

SMALL POSITIVE QUALITIES

WATER ELEMENT

SMALL POSITIVE QUALITIES

WATER ELEMENT

SMALL POSITIVE QUALITIES

WATER ELEMENT

SMALL POSITIVE QUALITIES

WATER ELEMENT

SMALL POSITIVE QUALITIES

WATER ELEMENT

SMALL POSITIVE QUALITIES

WATER ELEMENT

SMALL POSITIVE QUALITIES

WATER ELEMENT

SMALL POSITIVE QUALITIES

WATER ELEMENT

SMALL POSITIVE QUALITIES

WATER ELEMENT

MEDIUM POSITIVE QUALITIES

WATER ELEMENT

MEDIUM POSITIVE QUALITIES

WATER ELEMENT

MEDIUM POSITIVE QUALITIES

WATER ELEMENT

MEDIUM POSITIVE QUALITIES

WATER ELEMENT

MEDIUM POSITIVE QUALITIES

WATER ELEMENT

MEDIUM POSITIVE QUALITIES

WATER ELEMENT

MEDIUM POSITIVE QUALITIES

WATER ELEMENT

MEDIUM POSITIVE QUALITIES

WATER ELEMENT

MEDIUM POSITIVE QUALITIES

WATER ELEMENT

MEDIUM POSITIVE QUALITIES

WATER ELEMENT

LARGE POSITIVE QUALITIES

WATER ELEMENT

LARGE POSITIVE QUALITIES

WATER ELEMENT

LARGE POSITIVE QUALITIES

WATER ELEMENT

LARGE POSITIVE QUALITIES

WATER ELEMENT

LARGE POSITIVE QUALITIES

WATER ELEMENT

LARGE POSITIVE QUALITIES

WATER ELEMENT

LARGE POSITIVE QUALITIES

WATER ELEMENT

LARGE POSITIVE QUALITIES

WATER ELEMENT

LARGE POSITIVE QUALITIES

WATER ELEMENT

LARGE POSITIVE QUALITIES

AIR ELEMENT

SMALL POSITIVE QUALITIES

AIR ELEMENT

SMALL POSITIVE QUALITIES

AIR ELEMENT

SMALL POSITIVE QUALITIES

AIR ELEMENT

SMALL POSITIVE QUALITIES

AIR ELEMENT

SMALL POSITIVE QUALITIES

AIR ELEMENT

SMALL POSITIVE QUALITIES

AIR ELEMENT

SMALL POSITIVE QUALITIES

AIR ELEMENT

SMALL POSITIVE QUALITIES

AIR ELEMENT

SMALL POSITIVE QUALITIES

AIR ELEMENT

SMALL POSITIVE QUALITIES

AIR ELEMENT

MEDIUM POSITIVE QUALITIES

AIR ELEMENT

MEDIUM POSITIVE QUALITIES

AIR ELEMENT

MEDIUM POSITIVE QUALITIES

AIR ELEMENT

MEDIUM POSITIVE QUALITIES

AIR ELEMENT

MEDIUM POSITIVE QUALITIES

AIR ELEMENT

MEDIUM POSITIVE QUALITIES

AIR ELEMENT

MEDIUM POSITIVE QUALITIES

AIR ELEMENT

MEDIUM POSITIVE QUALITIES

AIR ELEMENT

MEDIUM POSITIVE QUALITIES

AIR ELEMENT

MEDIUM POSITIVE QUALITIES

AIR ELEMENT

LARGE POSITIVE QUALITIES

AIR ELEMENT

LARGE POSITIVE QUALITIES

AIR ELEMENT

LARGE POSITIVE QUALITIES

AIR ELEMENT

LARGE POSITIVE QUALITIES

AIR ELEMENT

LARGE POSITIVE QUALITIES

AIR ELEMENT

LARGE POSITIVE QUALITIES

AIR ELEMENT

LARGE POSITIVE QUALITIES

AIR ELEMENT

LARGE POSITIVE QUALITIES

AIR ELEMENT

LARGE POSITIVE QUALITIES

AIR ELEMENT

LARGE POSITIVE QUALITIES

FIRE ELEMENT

SMALL POSITIVE QUALITIES

FIRE ELEMENT

SMALL POSITIVE QUALITIES

FIRE ELEMENT

SMALL POSITIVE QUALITIES

FIRE ELEMENT

SMALL POSITIVE QUALITIES

FIRE ELEMENT

SMALL POSITIVE QUALITIES

FIRE ELEMENT

SMALL POSITIVE QUALITIES

FIRE ELEMENT

SMALL POSITIVE QUALITIES

FIRE ELEMENT

SMALL POSITIVE QUALITIES

FIRE ELEMENT

SMALL POSITIVE QUALITIES

FIRE ELEMENT

SMALL POSITIVE QUALITIES

FIRE ELEMENT

MEDIUM POSITIVE QUALITIES

FIRE ELEMENT

MEDIUM POSITIVE QUALITIES

FIRE ELEMENT

MEDIUM POSITIVE QUALITIES

FIRE ELEMENT

MEDIUM POSITIVE QUALITIES

FIRE ELEMENT

MEDIUM POSITIVE QUALITIES

FIRE ELEMENT

MEDIUM POSITIVE QUALITIES

FIRE ELEMENT

MEDIUM POSITIVE QUALITIES

FIRE ELEMENT

MEDIUM POSITIVE QUALITIES

FIRE ELEMENT

MEDIUM POSITIVE QUALITIES

FIRE ELEMENT

MEDIUM POSITIVE QUALITIES

FIRE ELEMENT

LARGE POSITIVE QUALITIES

FIRE ELEMENT

LARGE POSITIVE QUALITIES

FIRE ELEMENT

LARGE POSITIVE QUALITIES

FIRE ELEMENT

LARGE POSITIVE QUALITIES

FIRE ELEMENT

LARGE POSITIVE QUALITIES

FIRE ELEMENT

LARGE POSITIVE QUALITIES

FIRE ELEMENT

LARGE POSITIVE QUALITIES

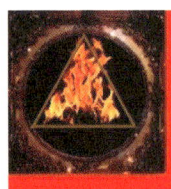

FIRE ELEMENT

LARGE POSITIVE QUALITIES

FIRE ELEMENT

LARGE POSITIVE QUALITIES

FIRE ELEMENT

LARGE POSITIVE QUALITIES

15604630R00075

Printed in Germany
by Amazon
Distribution